C is for Centennial

A Colorado Alphabet

Written by Louise Doak Whitney and Illustrated by Helle Urban

Sleeping Bear Press
310 North Main Street
P.O. Box 20
Chelsea, MI 48118
www.sleepingbearpress.com

Printed and bound in Canada.

10 9 8 7 6 5 4 3 2 1

Library of Congress Cataloging-in-Publication Data

Whitney, Louise D.
C is for centennial : a Colorado alphabet / by Louise D. Whitney ;
illustrated by Helle Urban.
p. cm.
Summary: Presents information about the state of Colorado in an
alphabetical arrangement.
ISBN 1-58536-058-9
1. Colorado—Juvenile literature. 2. English
language—Alphabet—Juvenile literature. [1. Colorado. 2. Alphabet.]
I. Urban, Helle, ill. II. Title.
F776.3 .W48 2002
978.8—dc21   2002004300

Gleaves, this book is for you.
You were dreaming of Colorado and I was dreaming of you!
For Ian, Alasdair, and Andrew—Dream of the
mountains, boys, and reach for the sky!
I will love you all forever.

For my parents, Bob and Martha,
they dreamed of Colorado and made it home.
May you rest in peace—dream now with each other again.

Thank you, Heather Hughes and Sleeping Bear Press.

LOUISE DOAK WHITNEY

To my loving husband and my darling daughter Amber,
thank you for your love and support.
Thank you, Heather Hughes and Sleeping Bear Press,
for the opportunity to illustrate this book.
It was a pleasure to do!

HELLE URBAN

Tiny flowers and lichen cling
to life on peaks soaring high.
A is for Alpine high, bright, and clear—
cold land between tree and sky.

The land above the trees, or the alpine zone, is the highest mountain land in Colorado. Since much of its land is alpine, Colorado has the highest mean elevation of any state. In fact 75% of the land in America that is over 10,000 feet is in Colorado! The plants and animals that live in the alpine zone are tough and sturdy. They have adapted to high winds, a short growing season, and the cold temperatures of the alpine life zone. If you hike above the trees, you may see a little pika scampering among the rocks and boulders. Pikas are small animals that are related to rabbits.

A is also for aquamarine, the Colorado state gem. Ranging from bright blue to pale blue and deep aquamarine green in color, it can be found in the mountains.

A is also for the city of Aspen. Before it was home to skiing, Aspen was a silver mining camp. The largest silver nugget ever mined in North America was found in Aspen. It weighed 1,840 pounds, the size of a small car. In 1936, the Highlands Bavarian ski resort started the first downhill ski run in Colorado, charging people a dime to ride the lift.

Aa

The Colorado blue spruce is a beautiful tree that was first named on Pikes Peak in 1862. It is an evergreen tree, which means it never loses its foliage. Its blue-green color is caused by the presence of waxes on the needles. It is a popular tree and prized all over the world.

B is also for "Buffalo Bill" (William Frederick Cody, 1846-1917). He was one of the Wild West's most colorful characters and folk heroes. His many careers included Pony Express rider, scout, and buffalo hunter, and his grave is on Lookout Mountain just west of Denver.

B b

B is for Blue spruce,
   Colorado's state tree.
   It blankets the mountains
   with blue-green majesty.

Col. W.F. Cody "Buffalo Bill"

Colorado is known as the Centennial State because it became the 38th state in 1876—100 years after the Declaration of Independence was signed. Did you know that the name Colorado means "colored red"? The Spanish gave the name to the Colorado River, which flows through canyons of red stone. Many of the rocks and much of the soil in Colorado are red.

C is also for the colors of the state flag. It can be said that the blue, red, white, and gold colors of the state flag symbolize certain natural wonders: gold for sunshine; white for the state's snow-capped mountains; red for the color of the earth; and blue for Colorado's clear blue skies.

C is for Colorado,
the colorful, Centennial State.
    We have high mountains and broad plains
and a history that makes us great.

STATE · OF · COLORADO

NIL SINE NUMINE

1876

The tallest sand dunes in America are found at the Great Sand Dunes National Monument and Preserve. The dunes can reach 700 feet and stand in the shadow of the Sangre de Cristo mountains. At night you might hear the coyotes talking to each other and in the early morning you might see pronghorn antelope grazing.

From rock and wind and water come Dunes for the letter D.
Shifting sands to climb and explore, the Great Sand Dunes you must see!

D
d

E is for Mt. Elbert,
   Colorado's highest peak.
When you climb to the top,
   you're over 14,000 feet.

ENOS MILLS CLIMBING TREE - 1915

There are 54 mountains in Colorado that are over 14,000 feet above sea level. Some people have climbed them all! There are more than 1,000 peaks over 10,000 feet high.

E is also for Enos Mills, who is known as the "Father of Rocky Mountain National Park." Enos was a naturalist who persuaded Congress to establish Rocky Mountain National Park in 1915. This park is the most popular tourist spot in Colorado. Here you can hike the trails and look for wildlife such as deer, elk, bighorn sheep, mountain goats, bald eagles, marmots, and black bear.

F is for the Four Corners.
   Put your hands and feet just so.
You'll be amazed to be in Colorado
      and in Utah, Arizona, and New Mexico!

The Four Corners Monument is fun to visit. Here you can be in four states (Colorado, Arizona, Utah, and New Mexico) at one time. It is the only place in the United States where you can be in four states at the same time! It is in the southwestern corner of the Ute Mountain Indian Reservation.

F is also for fossil. In the Florissant Fossil Beds National Monument, located in a mountain valley west of Pikes Peak, there are fossils of 1,100 species of prehistoric creatures that lived in a sequoia forest 35 million years ago. Volcanic eruptions buried the area, each time preserving a moment in natural history. Florissant Fossil Beds National Monument was designated as a national monument in 1969. The stegosaurus is the state fossil of Colorado.

Have you ever seen a Sleeping Giant
Kissing Camels, a Toad and Toadstool?
If you haven't...

Then you must visit the Garden of the Gods:
It begins with the letter **G**.
A place where geology comes alive,
full of red sandstone sculpture and mystery.

G g

The Garden of the Gods in Colorado Springs is indeed a land of mystery. Imagine if the sandstone sculptures could speak! They would tell tales of the petroglyphs left by the Ute Indians, or the trappers and traders who stopped there to camp, or the gold seekers who carved their names into the rock, and the settlers who came to live in the shadow of the magnificent sculptures.

G also stands for the grasses that grace the plains with their wavelike movements. The two most common types of grasses in Colorado are grama and buffalo. Blue grama grass is the state grass of Colorado. It is native to the state and grows on both sides of the Continental Divide.

In 1969, Mo Siegel gathered wild herbs in the forest and canyons around Aspen and Boulder and began making them into healthful teas. This was the beginning of Celestial Seasonings, which has since grown to be the largest herbal tea company in North America. With names like Sleepytime, Red Zinger, and Mint Magic, Celestial Seasonings has created healthy, flavorful beverages for all to enjoy.

H is also for Hovenweep National Monument, near the Colorado-Utah border. It is the site of five prehistoric Puebloan-era ruins that were once villages built by the Anasazi. Here you can see several small square towers built along the canyon rim and at the canyon bottom. While no one knows the purpose of these structures, they are unique to Hovenweep. Maybe you'll be the person to uncover what these mysterious ruins meant to the early people who built them.

H

H is for the Herbal teas
that Celestial Seasonings brews.
Sleepytime or Red Zinger—
They're all tasty, so you choose!

HOVENWEEP NATIONAL MONUMENT

The Towers of Hovenweep

I i

Insect starts with the letter I.
Our state insect is the Hairstreak Butterfly.
Fluttery, beautiful, and delicate—
watch for it when it flies by!

The lovely Hairstreak Butterfly's habitat is nearly limited to Colorado, making it a perfect choice for our state insect. A group of schoolchildren promoted the idea of having the butterfly be the state insect and so it was chosen in 1996. The Hairstreak proudly displays a multitude of colors that remind us of colorful Colorado! There is green for evergreen trees, purple for the columbine, orange for aspen in autumn, black for coal, and white for snow. The male butterfly only lives 4-5 days.

I is also for the beautiful Indian paintbrush—a red flower that blooms in June. Its spiky-looking foliage gives it the appearance of a paintbrush. Imagine being able to paint the world red with the brush of the flower!

The Rocky Mountain bighorn sheep is the state symbol and animal of Colorado. They usually live in the high country and are named for their distinctive horns that curve from front to back and then toward the front again. These sheep have an amazing ability to climb the steep crags of the mountains and they have perfect balance. Look closely and you might be lucky to see one the next time you go hiking!

J is also for juniper—a tree that is common in Colorado. Native Americans used the cones of some species as food. Junipers have a pleasant scent and that is why the lumber is prized for chests and closets. The berries are used as a flavor in cooking.

J j

Now we come to the letter J—
Jumping bighorn sheep.
Go high into the Rockies and see how
over creeks and boulders they will leap.

K is for Krummholz.
Pines high upon the peaks will show
how low and dense and twisted
crooked wood at tree line can grow.

Krummholz is a German word for "crooked wood." High up on the peaks where the weather is harsh, the tops of the trees will often break off when frozen and the wood becomes crooked as it continues to grow. This makes krummholz trees twisted and gnarled. You'll see the krummholz when you hike near tree line.

K is also for Kayaking or river running, a sport that flourishes in the rivers throughout Colorado. When water flows down steep mountains, it forms rapids or whitewater that kayakers love. Colorado is the headwater of more rivers than any other state: the Arkansas, South Platte, Republican, Colorado, Rio Grande, and North Platte rivers all begin in Colorado.

M is for Mesa Verde—
Pueblo, kiva, and cliff dwelling.
An ancient people called it home,
long before Columbus set sailing.

Mesa Verde, a national park, means "green table," and was home to the Anasazi, the early ancestors of the Pueblo Indians. It was the first park founded to protect the history of Native Americans. Nearly 1,000 years ago, the Anasazi built homes under the earth that sheltered them. Later they added kivas* and pueblos. About 800 years ago they moved up into the cliff dwellings. You can visit these today and imagine what life must have been like long, long ago in Colorado.

M is also for Mt. McClellan, a peak that is 14,007 feet above sea level. If you climb this peak or take the railway to the top you can see one-sixth of the entire state and see 106 of the state's tallest mountains.

*A kiva is a room where special religious ceremonies take place.

m
M

The lark bunting is a migratory bird that arrives home in Colorado in April after wintering in warmer climes farther south. Watch for them perched on fence posts whistling their favorite song.

Leadville also begins with the letter **L**. Located in the heart of the Colorado Rockies, it is America's highest city with an elevation of over 10,000 feet above sea level. Leadville was a bustling place during the 1860 Pikes Peak gold and 1875 silver rushes.

L is also the first letter of the town named Loveland. Here every year on Valentine's Day valentine cards from all over the United States are post-marked with "Loveland."

L is for the Lark bunting.
Colorado's state bird sings
from atop a fence-post perch,
a song that happiness brings.

LEADVILLE
ELEVATION 10,188'
HIGHEST CITY IN AMERICA

Nestled deep in Cheyenne Mountain N
is NORAD, beginning with an N.
On Christmas Eve they keep watch
for the journey of Santa to begin.

Deep within Cheyenne Mountain near Colorado Springs is NORAD—the North American Aerospace Defense Command. NORAD is a joint American and Canadian venture to protect our airspace. Years ago a newspaper article misprinted a phone number for children to call to find out where Santa was—it was the NORAD number, and since then every Christmas Eve, NORAD uses its sophisticated computer technology to track Santa Claus and his reindeer. You can call, too!

N is also for the national parks, monuments, forest, and grassland in Colorado that preserve our beautiful land. One-third of the land in Colorado is owned by the U.S. government. Denver has the largest park system in the U.S., with 205 city parks and 20,000 acres of parkland in the nearby mountains.

n
N

In 1893 American poetess Katharine Lee Bates was inspired to write *America the Beautiful* while at the summit of Pikes Peak. If you don't think you could climb the very steep 13 miles of the Barr Trail, you could take the cog railway (the highest in the world) to the summit.

O is also for Ouray, a former gold town named after a Ute Indian chief. It is known as the "Little Switzerland of America" because of its stunning location in the San Juan Mountains. Ouray is at the halfway point on the Million Dollar Highway, U.S. 550. It is hard to know if that name refers to the millions of dollars from gold that came from the nearby mines, or perhaps the cost of rebuilding the road, or maybe the million dollar views, as it ranks among the nation's most spectacular highways. Ouray has one of the few parks in the world dedicated to the sport of ice climbing.

O beautiful...

the Beautiful

for spacious skies
amber waves of grain
mountain majesties
the fruited plain!
America!

And

his

O is for "O Beautiful
  for spacious skies, for amber waves of grain."
Katharine saw it all before her
  "above the fruited plain."

Pp

Pony Express begins with a **P**.
Brave young riders rode hard and long
to deliver mail throughout the West,
on horses swift, sleek, and strong.

From 1860-1861, the Pony Express was the way mail was delivered to the West. Young men would ride their horses hard and long through all types of weather conditions to deliver mail to the early residents of Colorado. The first Pony Express station in Colorado was founded at Julesburg.

Colorado has many words that begin with **P** including prairie, peak, and plateau. The prairie or plains of Colorado, east of the mountains, comprise two-fifths of the state. The peaks in Colorado make up another two-fifths of the state. The plateaus of Colorado are west of the mountains and make up one-fifth of the state.

Another **P** word is Pawnee Buttes and National Grassland. The Pawnee Buttes are twin white sandstone formations that rise 250 feet above the plains. Many early animals made their homes here as seen by the fossil skeletons. Today the buttes are home to many nesting birds such as raptors, hawks, falcons, and kestrels.

The city of Denver is the capital of Colorado, where elected representatives meet to make the laws. The bright, shiny capitol dome is painted with pure gold leaf! Can you find the mile-high step on the capitol marking 5,280 feet? Denver is also home to Colfax Avenue, which is the longest street in America.

The Molly Brown house in Denver was the home of Maggie "Molly" Brown, the heroine of the Titanic. The Broadway musical and movie, *The Unsinkable Molly Brown*, is a fictionalized account of her life. She was the wife of Johnny "JJ" Brown. He struck it rich one day and built a fancy mansion in Denver. You can visit their house and see how Molly and JJ lived. What color do you think was Molly's favorite?

Q q

Q is for the 'Queen City of the Rockies':
That's Denver, the "Mile High City."
Larimer Square, a golden dome,
and Molly Brown's house—all places to see!

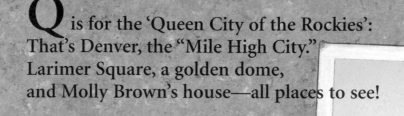

THE MOLLY BROWN HOUSE MUSEUM

LARIMER SQUARE

PRORODEO HALL OF FAME

R is for the Rockies,
the mountains of our state—
        or Rodeo, Roof, and Royal Gorge.
We live at heaven's gate!

The major mountain system of North America, the Rocky Mountains are usually divided into five sections, with the Southern Rockies running through New Mexico, Colorado, and southern Wyoming. The Southern Rockies are the system's highest section and Mt. Elbert in Colorado is the highest peak.

Rodeo begins with **R**. Colorado claims to have held the first rodeo in the nation in 1869 in Deer Trail and every year Denver hosts the largest rodeo, the National Western Stock Show and Rodeo. Be sure and visit the ProRodeo Hall of Fame and Museum of the American Cowboy in Colorado Springs.

R is also for Roof: Colorado is often called the "Roof of North America" because of all the high mountain peaks in this one state.

Royal Gorge is spanned by the highest suspension bridge in the world. It rises up 1,053 feet above the Arkansas River.

R r

Square dancing is the state folk dance of Colorado. Many communities hold square dances every Saturday evening. The female dancers wear brightly colored skirts and the partners whirl each other around the dance floor.

Springs also starts with **S**. Colorado has many springs: natural water sources that are hot and healing. Glenwood Springs is perhaps the most famous—it has the world's largest hot-spring pool. It is longer than a football field! Other Colorado cities that boast springs include Colorado Springs, Manitou Springs, Eldorado Springs, Pagosa Springs, Steamboat Springs, Hot Sulphur Springs, and Idaho Springs.

Do you ride a bicycle? Is it a Schwinn? **S** also stands for Schwinn bicycles made in Boulder since 1895.

S s

S is for Square dancing.
We love to "do-si-do."
So colorful the whirling,
around and 'round we go.

Our T is for Baby Doe Tabor—
the Silver Queen was she.
The mining town of Leadville
gave her a place in history.

Baby Doe Tabor's real name was Elizabeth McCourt before she married Horace Tabor. He was the owner of the mine known as the Matchless. This mine had the richest silver lode in Colorado history. Even though Baby Doe and Horace made more money than they could spend, they both died penniless.

T is also for Trail Ridge Road, U.S. 34, which climbs over the Continental Divide. Its highest point just over 12,000 feet, Trail Ridge Road is the highest highway in the United States.

Telluride starts with a T and it's the festival city of Colorado. The Telluride Jazz, Bluegrass, and Film Festivals all make this city a great place to visit during the summer.

T t

The United States Air Force Academy is where students go to college and learn to be officers in the U. S. Air Force. Many also learn to fly. The academy has more visitors here than any other man-made place in the Pikes Peak region. Be sure and look for the spires of the cadet chapel; they can be seen from miles away.

U is also for the U.S. Mint. It's where coin money is made. There are several manufacturing facilities around the country, including one in Denver. What a rich place to visit!

u
U

U is for the United States Air Force Academy,
with a chapel and spires so high.
Young men and women come here to learn
to soar above the clouds and fly.

V
V

V is for the village of Vail,
where America loves to ski.
Jump on the lift and down you go—
such a thrill, you'll say "Wheeeee!"

Vail is known as one of the best ski resorts in the world. It was designed as a European-style ski village and it opened in 1962. Here you can not only ski, but in the summer you can visit the Betty Ford Alpine Gardens, the highest public gardens in North America.

V is also for Victor, a city that was called "The City of Mines" because of the rich gold mines that once flourished there. One of Victor's famous residents was Lowell Thomas, a journalist and world traveler who worked at the *Victor Record*.

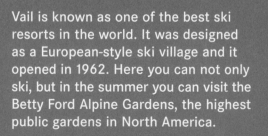

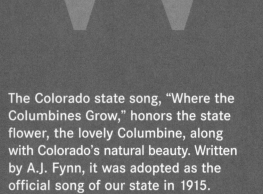

"Where the Columbines Grow"

Where the snowy peaks gleam in the
Above the dark forests of pine,
And the wild foaming waters dash
Toward lands where the tr...
Where the sc...
Resp...
...
The...
...
'Tis...
Ove...
...

The Colorado state song, "Where the Columbines Grow," honors the state flower, the lovely Columbine, along with Colorado's natural beauty. Written by A.J. Fynn, it was adopted as the official song of our state in 1915.

Another **W** word is the White River National Forest. It was once the favorite hunting ground of the Ute Indians and later the settlers of the Wild West. Today you can visit wilderness areas with fanciful names such as Flat Tops, Eagles Nest, Hunter-Fryingpan, Holy Cross, Ptarmigan Peak, Raggeds, and Maroon Bells-Snowmass, to go backpacking, mountain climbing, fishing, and big-game hunting.

W is also for the Wolf Creek Pass, one of the highest and steepest passes in the United States. It was also one of the last highways in Colorado to be paved.

Our state song begins with a **W**.
"Where the Columbines Grow" is its name.
We raise our voices with pride
as we sing of Colorado's fame.

X

X is for cross (X)-country skiing.
In the back country we will go.
As soon as the white flakes begin to fall
we'll swish and swoosh through the snow.

Cross-country skiing, which is often abbreviated with an **X**, is a favorite winter sport in Colorado. There is an abundance of trails to choose from, some are groomed and many are wild.

X is also the way in which mines are noted on old Colorado maps. The **X** is made with a pickax and shovel and marked the site of important gold and silver mines in the state.

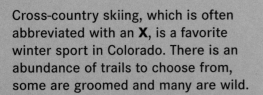

MAP OF THE REGION 1884

ROUTES

COLORADO SPRINGS

Y y

Y is for Yucca, a poky, spiky plant,
and Yampa River and Plateau.
Only a few Colorado names begin with Y
but these are fun to know.

Yuccas are evergreen plants common
in Colorado. The Plains Indians,
Arapaho, Cheyenne, and Sioux used
just about every part of the yucca
either in food, baskets, or soap. When
in bloom, the yucca has pretty white
flowers.

It was along the Yampa River that the
springs gushing forth became known
as Steamboat Springs. Although the
springs are calm now, in the old days
you could hear the steamboat-like "chug,
chug, chug" noises for miles around.

Good ole Zeb Pike.
His first name starts with Z.
"America's mountain" has his name—
Pikes Peak to you and me.

ZEBULON M. PIKE
1779-1813

CHEYENNE MOUNTAIN ZOO

Amber petting a miniature pony at Cheyenne Mountain Zoo.

Zebulon M. Pike was the explorer who was charged with mapping the region in his expedition in 1806. Zebulon never did make it to the top of Pikes Peak—he thought it could not be climbed! Today, Pikes Peak is the most famous mountain in Colorado, and is known as "America's mountain." Every year more than 250,000 people enjoy the summit view.

Z is for Zoo—the Cheyenne Mountain Zoo—the only mountain zoo in the United States. At an elevation of 6,800 feet, you can learn about and see over 650 animals (representing some 142 species) and enjoy the great views of Colorado Springs, too. With 177 births since 1954, the zoo's giraffe breeding program is one of the largest in the world. Zounds!

Z z

Colorful Colorado Facts!

1. Why is Colorado known as the Centennial State?

2. What is the state fossil of Colorado?

3. What does the German word Krummholz mean?

4. What city in Colorado is the highest city in the United States?

5. Who wrote the song *America the Beautiful*?

6. What city in Colorado is known as the "Mile High City"?

7. What is the name of Colorado's highest mountain?

8. What does Mesa Verde mean and what is it?

9. How was mail delivered to the West in the early days?

10. What is the major mountain system that runs through Colorado?

Answers

1. It became a state in 1876—100 years after the Declaration of Independence was signed.

2. The stegosaurus is the state fossil of Colorado.

3. It means "crooked wood" and refers to the twisted and crooked trees growing up on the high mountain peaks.

4. With an elevation over 10,000 feet above sea level, Leadville is America's highest city.

5. Katharine Lee Bates wrote the song after being inspired by a visit to Pikes Peak.

6. Denver

7. Mt. Elbert

8. It means "green table" and was home to the Anasazi, early ancestors of the Pueblo Indians. It is now a national park.

9. By Pony Express

10. The Rocky Mountains

Reference List

Celestial Seasonings Web site: www.celestialseasonings.com

Cheyenne Mountain Zoo Web site: www.cmzoo.org

Colorado State Government Web site: www.colorado.gov (as well as official links, including State Archives)

Colorado State Web site: www.colorado.com

Encyclopaedia Britannica, 1998

Harris, Richard. *Hidden Colorado* (Ulysses Press: Berkeley, CA 2000).

Laine, Don and Barbara. *Frommer's Colorado* (Simon & Schuster: NY, 1997).

Leadville Web site: www.leadvilleusa.com

Metzger, Stephen. *Colorado Handbook* (Chico, CA: Moon Publications, 1999).

Pikes Peak Web site: www.pikes-peak.com

Schwinn's Web site: www.schwinn.com

Time Almanac, 2001

U.S. State Parks Web site: www.parks.state.co.us

Webster's New Collegiate Dictionary, 1981, and www.websters.com

Whitney, Gleaves. *Colorado Front Range: A Landscape Divided* (Johnson Books: Boulder, CO 1983)

World Almanac & Book of Facts, 2002

World Book Encyclopedia, 2000